the lightbulb has stigmata

Helen Fletcher

The Onslaught Press

Published in Oxford by The Onslaught Press
11 Ridley Road, OX4 2QJ
October 2016

ISBN: **978-0-9956225-0-0**

Typeset in Akira Kobayashi's **Din Next** & Christ Burke's **FF Celeste**,
designed & edited by **Mathew Staunton**

Printed by Lightning Source

for my daughters, April and Mila

The phone box where I argued with your father
now houses an automated external defibrillator.

+

AEDs don't let their users choose
the timings of the shocks.
The receiver is lifted
and dropped.

-

'Can you still hear me?
Call me back.'

Part 1: He points to his heart

Part 2: He points to the sky

Part 3: The Welcome

Part 1:
He points to his heart

I met my own body on a park bench in Paris

'I have sat here so long,' my slumped head said,
'spikenard has sprung from my tears like Greek Helen.
Do you remember how his armpits smelled of roast chicken?
and his skin was smoother after he'd come?'

'I try not to think of him,' I said,
'it's not as hard for me—he loved me less.'
Then we didn't speak. I hovered by the bench.
'Where have you been?' my muffled voice asked me.

'Just floating through the city looking into houses:
I saw a man writing music and a woman marking mathsbooks.
He adjusted all the chords and shyly gazed at her,
these two worked through the night.

'And I saw her corrections were copied in the clouds—
the rings and ticks and crosses joined up to look like lambs,
and I saw his playing create sound-waves
which nudged each new-born shape across the sky.'

Then my face looked up at me. 'Pareidolia,' she said,
'I have often seen things that aren't there;
I'd hear Shhh when he said Shut up.
I didn't say Stop.' We both remembered.

I saw the skin under my eyes was thin.
'Anyway,' my body said, 'I need a haircut and some breakfast.'
And standing up, she stubbed a weed out with her boot
and, cocking her chin slightly, beckoned me to come along.

Chinese Legend

Where is the way?
He points to the sky.
Where is the sky?
He points to his heart.

Hospital Coffee

Sometimes doctors come into the café bloody.
We're told not to serve surgeons if they're still in scrubs, but I serve them;
the doctors are so busy, they need to be kept going.

You can hear the hepatologist a long way off:
he sings and swears and talks to himself loudly—
it could be blustering shyness.
I get his large Americano ready,
he always acts surprised to see it waiting for him,
he forgets his stamp card so we keep one behind the till,
he buys coffees for his students sometimes.

The machine screams into the milk.
He has blood on his shoe-covers.

'Ah, nectar!' he says, leaving.
I want to ask him how the liver purifies everything that goes into a man
and how he fixes it
but he needs a break.

I used to read Scripture and there is a chaplaincy here.
But the services never fit my shifts and it's for patients really.

A woodlouse is neither a proud worm nor a heavenly butterfly

I am a hiding thing.
I don't have any hinterwings
for enforced metamorphoses.

You say you'll be my hiding place—
that inside your red cave, flame-shaped wounds
there's dead wood for me to chew.
Would you not flinch from fourteen feet creeping into you?

I will make you sick.

The lightbulb has stigmata

The lightbulb has stigmata.
I don't know if you can see on Skype?
I used to get so scared at night before I went to bed—
when the road went quiet, I'd see
shadows flicker in the bathroom.
It's been such a comfort to me since Simon died.

It drips from the hall light, hanging from the ceiling.
Hang on, I'll move the camera.
I can't show friends here—it only starts at night
but with the time difference you're still up.
I switch off all the lights to go to bed and then it starts.
It's been such a comfort to me this year.

So, yesterday, after lying in bed listening,
I came downstairs and sat under the light
on the small circle of blood.
I felt it wet my nightie and I waited.
Nothing hit me. I tipped my head back
and looked up into the darkness.

I thought it would make me weep and weep
to sit there on our parquet floor,
where Simon fixed the shaky bricks of wood.
To stop, in the centre of the routes we took
from the front door to the kitchen,
from the living room to the loo . . .
Warm blood touched the bridge of my nose,
and rolled into my eyes, congealing them closed.

You know what he was like and he got even worse,
I couldn't say a thing that didn't make him angry.
He fell, going to the loo, and shouted, 'Pick me up!'—
you know I couldn't—and he screamed that I just didn't want to.
He was writhing on wet flooring
when I came back with our neighbour.

Blood ran down my head and let itself
fall into the joints of the hard floor.
I smiled because, out of nowhere,
I remembered making love here in our twenties—
but then I started to get cold
so I pulled on my fleece dressing-gown and made a cup of tea.
Do you think I should tell a priest?
You'll see it, anyway, next time you're here.

Deus Meus

Deus Meus
Exaudi me,
Deus meus
Suscipe me.
Deus meus,
Dios dies.
'Basta.
Basta,'
I have cried.

holy communion

inside the stainless steel chalice
she saw a face in a pool of rocking water
sono la via e
she always gives way

she doesn't say no
she was surprised men had wanted her
she had made her fiancée's face change
into five wounds weeping

holding the chalice she wanted
to duck to let parishioners
get back to their seats
but she also didn't want to drop it

and she was a clumsy person
la verità
she was always spilling drinks
on her cream carpet

she changed her mind
e la vita
even though it was too late
it was then she tipped the chalice

and helped herself
to her wobbling face

Cambridge Finals

The Tragedy paper wasn't trying to be ironic:
when you desire something with all your will,
it turns your vision visionary.
It was talking about Dante and didn't know
I wanted to succeed so badly I'd just seen my tutor
glide down the Cam on Shakespeare's first folio.
> White pages fluttered like sails in the wind,
> thick wooden paddle wheels spun,
> and her Siamese cats sat like sentinels round her,
> tails ticking slowly from side to side,
> as she had her roots done with my yellow highlighter.
> > I covered my head with post-its
> > and forgot how to tell the time.

Laughing in the Tragedy exam isn't encouraged.
The quartered clock struck honestly,
you have five minutes left.
> Someone brought me milk
> and strapped hands to my wrist.
> *Hands together pointing up*
> *means eat again or sleep.*
The tutor I loved like my mother glided past unsmiling,
I sat failing with victory ticks on my trainers,
I left everything on the table.

Ancient Greek Anger Management

Our squatters—the Eumenides—are judging us.
I get a bad breast-feeling they won't go away.
This court is now in session.
Do you swear to tell the truth?
I swear to remember my submission
to control these old women
he's refused to entertain.
You're beating yourself, they say.
They forget they were once wild Erinyes
who'd want to gauge out eyes with house keys.
This is another spike for his graphs:
my *chthonic tectonics.*
But he's right it's a fault, it's my fault,
a fault-line that condemns our home.

The Lamprey and the Lily

The Lamprey:

I've clung on by my teeth
but the sea has shattered me.
I've been dragged here upstream,
River Lily hold onto me.

Your flowers are mango yellow,
dragons swoop to drink from you,
you've not been bent by the current,
kings swim through your roots.

The salmon have outmanoeuvred me,
they don't feel the heavy sea,
now the long pool calls to me.
River Lily hold on to me.

The Lily:

I will
until the flood
my darling.

I will
until the river
dries.

Bloodless
I will
until you ride away.

The Way

A hillside and a kite.
The string slits his hand
    and when the handle snaps and the wind grabs,
the kite-string cuts the sky in half.

    Tummy, incubator, coffin
that she carries on her knees
    in their car to church.
From the removed cannula, the back of her hand bleeds.

Ora pro Laura

The spheres roll round:
the joyful decades,
the glorious decades,
the sorrowful decades,
decades of dead ends.

But there will come a time my dear
when children with armfuls of flowering branches
(leaving others with firewood for the mansions' fireplaces),
laughing and running from far away,
will come to bring the branches to your fingertips—
every circular rut of your digits
is a socket for matching ring of a blossoming tree
that makes pink snow in spring—
and they will fit perfectly and the sap will run
into your blood and your blood into the sap,
and your nails painted pearly pink will grow
into magnolia flowers to hold the branches.

Then the children up on ladders
will get apples and avocados
out of baskets to adorn you
and will make a full crown.

And all this won't be heavy
because you will be lying down by the water,
on your back by the beck by the walnut tree,
with your arms by your sides,
and you will let your hair down into the stream—
yes, the beauty parlour of Paradise!—
and let your roots get drenched,
with your palms to the sun.

Dream of a Man Giving Me Expensive Things

He said: 'When you hide your crying in the shower,
or blink back tears to love-songs
on long and empty Sunday afternoons,
or are surprised into weeping by sudden resemblances—
every time you dissolve into mists of tears
I gather them here
and set them into diamonds.
You have cried five pints of tears.
They roll down white stalactites,
and leave their pillars of salt behind,
casting stained glass flashes,
and making, with those of other people,
the columns of a crystal cathedral.
Let me give them back to you.

'I can't tell you exactly what to do.
Scatter some in a graveyard,
leave some by the water,
be sparing when it feels right,
sow the rest in someone's sky . . .'

The Box

She drove back with the box.
He had agreed to meet her.

'I have killed the vampire,' she said.
'I trapped it in the cloakroom,
backed into the kickboards.
I stapled shut its ears and nose
and sewed its eyes together,
I couldn't bear it staring at me.
It shrank to just an open mouth.
After a year, its teeth fell out,
the eye-teeth last, their roots
were like claw-settings for diamonds.
And now it's dead.'

'You can't change what you are,' he said,
'this is just a ring.'

Swarm

Some words that were said to me want blood:
they swarm inside my bow mouth
which tightens as I smile at him—

he pushes breath out his nose and looks down at his meal.
Good men sniff and don't say how they feel.

And now the words will lodge in him, till,
sitting at the kitchen table, years from now . . .
She won't deserve it, but neither did he
and the stories of another way are lies—

as if those words could ever have been trapped
in a tea tin by a traveller
on an old cart leaving town.

The Warning

The bar maid wiped her hands on aproned hips,
before picking an ice-cube off the floorboards.
She carried it back behind the bar
and let it slide into the bin.

I should, then, have picked up my suitcase and left.
She brought me a cappuccino and didn't ring it in,
she let me linger on the balcony edge of her bra,
as I drank the milky coffee through a straw.

Salt Marsh

God was two miles of fire
outside my bedroom window:
two miles high and ten feet wide.
He said, 'Walk with me on Burgh Marsh.'
I left my husband sleeping.

I walked with God on the marshes.
He led me over the gullies
towards the edge of the headland,
the estuary curled into steam.
Then he moved towards me,
flames charged up my legs and my nostrils,
shelled my contacts and shoved my feet
up a spiral stair of fire,
till I stood in the sky.

Flames reached out fingers around the neck of England;
Bowness was squeezed against North Shields,
Hadrian's Wall like broken beads fell into the sea.
I saw my house was burning,
I looked down into the twins' room,
God burned the cots round my daughters.
I screamed and swore at my God.
The cot rails burnt down like candles
on two birthday cakes,
but not a single flame touched them.
The girls slept on unscathed.

I woke on Port Carlisle's tide-mark in fog.
Tom appeared in Prada trainers.
I remembered us undressing here, years ago,
newly unfaithful.

'I'm scared,' I said, 'I haven't changed.'
The fog thickened and he moved towards me,
I felt his aftershave knock my brain.
He kissed me slowly on my forehead
and said, 'You'll see it through.'

He said, 'There was a Palaeolithic couple,
who were really scared of something coming,
and so they stalked and killed and skinned and stripped
and hacked for days, with low-grade blades,
pre-historic mammoths, and with the bones
they made their home. Here, in fact,
and they didn't just kill ten or twenty
but ninety six and from how the bones fell
you can tell their home had grown
from a low cage to a palisaded hall—
the walls were thick and made of hips
packed with driven skulls, ball joints stuffed the gaps
and one hundred and ninety two tusks
rose high from the ground, like torii gates,
to make a guarded passage to their bed.
Their fear made them great,
and it kept their children safe.'

In the freezing dawn I was shaking,
Tom stood up and sighed at the muck on his trainers.
Then he smiled and walked towards Anthorn,
where his grandparents had lodged prisoners of war,
in their farm-buildings on the salt marsh,
training them in basic flock-management.

Part 2:
He points to the sky

Boy's Drawing

He put a tree in the middle,
2 people lie under it,
near tents and scattered money too big for the scale.
A head looks out of a pink tent.
On flags there are representations of stars
and primary colours.

6 bombs fall from planes. He pressed too hard
on a wing and you can see where the lead broke.
The tree is made of 28 Vs
like a probability tree of the possible outcomes.
A bird jumps out it.
Brown bullets fall through the branches
and dive towards the sleepers underneath;
they are hitting a leg, an arm, a chest,
a cheek and a smiley face—
but then again they might be eggs.

Cowrie Beach

He walks along the beach of bones,
the cowrie beach of outer bones,

on a thousand million little mouths
too small to listen to.

They adjust to his pressings
and kiss his paddling toes.

Tea with a Patients' Advocate

I want to say I know how it feels
To be held down in the night
And silenced
But that would be an inappropriate disclosure.
It's not like I'm in that young offenders institute,
Where a boy's wrist was broken
Because he wouldn't clean a toastie maker.
I can't complain
They made me safe
To be left.
In A&E, a nurse stayed with me,
Turned off the lights and talked about her son—
But then I was transferred.
I'd rather just stay quiet since I've had no more trouble,
I get ward-leave now at weekends,
I can wash that for you.

Kensington & Etruria

.

A boy popped out of a ploughed field in Etruria.
He told them about boundary stones, water systems
and town planning; about the faceless guardians of the dead
and the arrangement of the gleaming inner organs of a man.
That night he died upon the field and there they built their city.

..

The boy who served us came back with the bill.
We'd sent him out for cigarettes after our slow-cooked veal;
he ran along the King's Road and under the licensee's name.
In his homeland, he was made to be a slave
by a family whose status meant they couldn't own a field.

Birthday

Lift me out of the crypt and touch me.
Carry me down the street
to the steps of the town hall
and sit down with your sister.
Then I'll hear the things you're up to,
drooping on your legs I'll listen.
You were always that bit stronger.
And the afternoon will fly by,
to the songs of other families,
wrapped in the new shroud you'll bring,
you will pat me like a baby.
I was known so well by you,
filleted flesh from bone.
I thought I had enough love for us both.

()

Hidden chases have been cut
into the walls.
We lined ourselves up:

she shone

in our beginner's circuit,
like she does now, in his duplex.
Thomas, I miss her too.

Quebec, 1998

If a tree has to hold up an inch of ice along each branch
that's a force more than thrice its weight.
Boughs will be prized apart.

Orchards worth 3 billion dollars were lost,
where sugar ran up red trees,
and the moon guided old mum and dad's paths.

Allie can remember them in their twenties
and the house before the storm.
I never remember my parents as anything but middle-aged.

The man who cut the cross

had a bad job when you think about it—
cutting crucifixes from stripped timbers.
How smooth did he finish them?
Was his father a carpenter?
Did he hope to do great things?

But had he not done it well, had the cross collapsed,
would claw-hammers have set upon
the broken feet of a young man?
Christ twice crucified
in a botched Golgotha.

The Drowned

after David Harsent

The drowned came back to tell us there is nothing more.
They came from crooks of deep sea trees
where they can only keep the beat
of the music of the breaking sea.
Improvisation isn't for everyone
and no one held them on the beaches
or begged forgiveness for forgetting them—
it wasn't what was planned.
They were seen in the ocean
but there hadn't been any training
on how to bring them back to land.

It seems unlikely

when the boat he'd paid 5 grand for was full—
after the bombings in Aleppo and his girls' schools closed,
after living in a camp for a year and carrying
his 9 year-old across a country—
he swam alongside the boat, from Turkey to Greece.
Well, I suppose some men are that strong.
And the story has probably been changed for emotional impact,
it wouldn't actually have been alongside
and at the narrowest stretch it's only 2½ miles.
His wife got their 2 daughters and their 3 bags
out of the boat, where it stopped off the coast,
into the sea, over the rocks and onto the island without him.
(Some wives of strong men lose their strength.)

Wheelbarrow

Two newborn (male) calves
still wet
are pushed
to be fed
(dead)
to a snow leopard
through the gathered crowd.

Coniston Shore

We sat on this bench and fed the ducks and geese.
I felt his voice knock at my shoulder-blades.
We ate cheese sandwiches and felt each other's voices
move through the timber rails into our chests,
as though the slatted bench were ribs
and we its young, protected heart.
Now, sitting here alone,
holding on to the arm,
the wood is still across my back.
I am reducing, slowly, into a plaque
that can only say his name
and that he is gone.
I cannot move.
Nailed on.

Evening Song

'Don't wake up, my sleeping Jesus,
sleep upon the rocking sea.
God upon a pillow sleeping,
sweet dreams, love, of Galilee?

'I can see a storm approaching,
you've been working hard all day,
get some rest behind the netting,
now is not the time to pray.

'I am only ever tempor-
arily composed,' she sighed.
He is gorgeous when he's sleeping.
I am weeping at his side.

I Wash. You Dry.

I wash, you dry.
You wash, I dry.

I wash you,
I wash you,
I wash you,

dry.

I,
you.

I.

Winter Prayer

Another November, another December,
the burnt out embers of another year.

I sat in my bath in tears on my wedding night
and knew it wouldn't last;

the nicest thing his mother did was never ask
if we were having kids because we didn't manage it.

I'm not good on my own, I'm not one of those people,
it's just not how I thought my life would be;

with splinters of the holy tree,
God of what's left, kindle me.

Remorsels

She has shriked herself again
on thorns in someone else's boundary.
She upgrades to tupperware of her own
with lids that let no air get in.

Giant's Gob Induction

Yes, I am now fat-fat like my chief used to be.
Those neighbours moan till evening
as if they had no food—
something about light and hygiene,
they are very young.
But they're right, the mouth has dirty habits.
I was ecstatic at my first meal in here—
I ate through walls of beef from giant cows,
we all got drunk in dark wine
and I had never tasted chocolate.
I've learnt where to hide and you'll adjust,
a lot depends on where you come from.
I like to hear my giant's voice,
sometimes I stroke his gums,
and the only thing that makes me sick
is when they sing an old song of my people.
Slap me if you hear me crying, it's a stupid lullaby,
you're not from there, you won't believe
the things it makes me feel.

Stable Life

I need to go to Joseph's,
he knows what I need.
I need to go to Joseph's,
he knows where I've been.

To be neither broken in,
nor out of control:
half enclosed within a split-hinged
bolted stable door.

I will go to Joseph's,
he will run with me.
I'll go back to Joseph's.
I know what's good for me.

my mum re Julie Christie & *Doctor Zhivago*

the men in her life are very powerful
and she's lovely in it

He was still a schoolboy

when they swam to the island;
weeds stuck to her and she didn't say
she felt a snake hiding amongst them.
She sat down calmly and let him talk,
while its tail stubbed the small of her back
and its tongue tapped her halter-neck.
Of course it bit her and she screamed,
he killed it with his bare hands and feet.
She didn't care that it would hurt her.
Into the shade of fig trees, he carried her,
hand-shaped shadows played.
He had to find a boat.
When he came back she was giggling.

Looking onto West Walls, Carlisle

Today I am propped up by a Pot Noodle,
last week it was shower gel.
From the top corner of Paternoster Row,
I've seen grave-robbers and shoppers
cobble up the dirty snow.

I will be replaced by PVC,
for someone else to look through noble gas.
He lifts me up to spit on heads of passers-by.
Dealing feeds him.
Props change.

Mort Brod

after Jacob Polley

Death's bored in his nursery.
Leans his elbow on the skin of an hourglass drum.
Holds a hearth-brush against his collarbone as if it were a gun.

Part 3:
The Welcome

Lullaby Composed by a Conservation Worker

You will drive to see the ocean
and its algal blooms at night,
and how they light,
with glowing greens and blues,
the sides and fins of dolphins,
easing through them.

I brought your daddy soft fruit in hospital
and got him to accept the tubes.
He was like that badger,
trapped all night for vaccination—
sometimes they need to bite you.
It's just luck: the monstrousness
you'll meet, in yourself and out there,
how careful the controls will be.
Still, when I see fox-cubs playing
it makes me cry and, child, I am not lying
when I sing about the dolphins
and their bioluminescent greens and blues.

Seventh Day

On the seventh day God locked his head
into the neck and shoulder of his creation
and rested his face against the breathing world.

The sculptor holds that gods are made to rest on:
she cut wide the Belgian blue stone ballerino
and fixed the twisted marble in a fish lift.

She set them sleeping in the streaming grasses,
in the botanic gardens,
by the clawed frogs' pond.

Eel

Since I became an eel
I find it easier to squee-
ze into portholes to meet
captains and their crew.
It wouldn't suit everyone,
the depths that I
can swim to.
I grow into a wave
that crashes on my prey
and pushes them to my feasting halls.
Now I captain ships.
I have jaws that can break bricks.
I don't need arms to hold me,
I have found my resting place.
A conger is not a monster,
to thrive is not bad taste.

For an Undergraduate

If I could sit on your bed
and whisper to you, 'Stay',
would you look up at me
and see I understand?

You had incomplete advice
and too many invitations
and some chances are too great
to make the most of.

Then I'd offer you a latte
and a wrap from Prêt à Manger,
and we'd walk to the library,
past the limes and spiralling climbers.

Awn

Lifted up and spun around
in the best hay barn
a 5 mil rye awn falls.

As this was being repeated,
with other broken crests
that floated golden in the beams,

my eyes tracked to the door.
I'd have kissed the lintel,
if I were taller.

The Welcome

The children of the mansions are at the garden parties,
Everyone wears sun-cream here.
Come down whenever you're ready,
Or not at all, today.
You don't have to crop the currants in the fruit cages.

You've come a long way,
You have done well.
It is so hard to leave, I know.

This is your room,
Choir is quarter to six, dinner is six thirty,
Tomorrow there's tea with your guardian at three.
There are more blankets in the cupboard.
I'm your key worker. I'm new as well.

Acknowledgements

Acknowledgments and thanks to the following publications and platforms:

The Frogmore Papers, In Daily Adelaide News,
The Interpreter's House, The Journal, New Writing Cumbria,
Pennine Platform, roymarshall.wordpress, Snakeskin,
South Bank Poetry, Southlight, Third Way.

'The lightbulb has stigmata' was performed at Theatre by the Lake, Keswick as part of Words by the Water Literature Festival, March 2016.

Special thanks to Mathew Staunton, Mary Robinson, Christopher Pilling, Julia Dias, Issie Abbott, Joe Crawford and Sam Fletcher.

Jewellery for author photograph by Culietta.

poetry & haiku titles from The Onslaught Press

Out of the Wilderness (2016) by Cathal Ó Searcaigh
with an introduction and translations by Gabriel Rosenstock

You Found a Beating Heart (2016) Nisha Bhakoo

ident (2016) Alan John Stubbs

I Wanna Make Jazz to You (2016) Moe Seager

Tea wi the Abbot (2016) Scots haiku by John McDonald
with transcreations in Irish by Gabriel Rosenstock

Judgement Day (2016) Gabriel Rosenstock

We Want Everything (2016) Moe Seager

to kingdom come (2016) edited by Rethabile Masilo

The Lost Box of Eyes (2016) Alan John Stubbs

Antlered Stag of Dawn (2015) Gabriel Rosenstock,
with translations by Mariko Sumikura & John McDonald

behind the yew hedge (2015) Mathew Staunton & Gabriel Rosenstock

Bumper Cars (2015) Athol Williams

Waslap (2015) Rethabile Masilo

Aistear Anama (2014) Tadhg Ó Caoinleáin

for the children of Gaza (2014)
edited by Mathew Staunton & Rethabile Masilo

Poison Trees (2014) Philippe Saltel & Mathew Staunton

Lightning Source UK Ltd.
Milton Keynes UK
UKOW02f0815011116
286592UK00002B/45/P